Poetic
Offerings

God's Way, His Truth, and Our Lives

Poetic
Offerings

God's Way, His Truth, and Our Lives

NAOMI TERRANELLA
RONALD TERRANELLA
DONALD TERRANELLA

Scripture taken from the New King James Version® Copyright© 1982 by Thomas Nelson. Used by permission. All rights reserved.

Printed in the United States of America
ISBN 978-1-967279-53-1 (hc)
ISBN 978-1-967279-52-4 (sc)
ISBN 978-1-967279-54-8 (e)

Library of Congress Control Number: 2022917316

22.07.2025

This book is printed on acid-free paper.

Blue Ink Media Solutions
1111B S Governors Ave
STE 7582 Dover,
DE 19904
www.blueinkmediasolutions.com

DEDICATION

To our mother, Ida, who loved God's Word, lived His Word,
and taught us the true meaning of love.

LOVE

LOVE SUFFERS LONG AND IS KIND; LOVE DOES
NOT ENVY. LOVE DOES NOT PARADE ITSELF, IS
NOT PUFFED UP; DOES NOT BEHAVE RUDELY,
DOES NOT SEEK ITS OWN, IS NOT PROVOKED,
THINKS NO EVIL; DOES NOT REJOICE IN
INIQUITY, BUT REJOICES IN TRUTH; BEARS
ALL THINGS, BELIEVES ALL THINGS, HOPES ALL
THINGS, ENDURES ALL THINGS.

AND NOW ABIDE FAITH, HOPE, LOVE, THESE
THREE; BUT THE GREATEST OF THESE IS LOVE.

1 CORINTHIANS 13:4–13

ACKNOWLEDGMENTS

OH COME. LET US SING TO THE LORD! LET
US SHOUT JOYFULLY TO THE ROCK OF OUR
SALVATION.

LET US COME BEFORE HIS PRESENCE WITH
THANKSGIVING: LET US SHOUT JOYFULLY TO
HIM WITH PSALMS.

PSALM 95:1–2

We are forever grateful to our family members who have supported us throughout this journey:

To Edwin Miller, who encouraged us to follow our dream and fulfill our purpose.

To our siblings, Carl, Terry, Valerie, and Timothy. Their unconditional, uplifting love guided our hearts.

To our spouses, Edwin, Portia, and Julie, who patiently understood our aspiration to serve God.

To our children, who inspire us and give us a reason to share God's love; so that it can be passed on for generations to come.

And most of all, we thank Almighty God for giving His endless blessings that made this book possible.

Table of Contents

A Better Man

Lord, make me a better man,
The one You intended when drawing the plan.

Hewn from the heart of a sturdy tree
With faith unbending, except at the knee.

Carved by the skill of Your mighty hand
With honor, not pride, to heed Your command.

Detailed by grasses of gentle hue,
Hearing my prayers to make me brand-new.

Paint me with righteousness, dress me in love,
Your marionette with strings from above.

DONALD TERRANELLA

A Christmas Cookie

Looking for some Christmas kicks,
She used her soul to mix
A big batch of cookies,
The whole world to fix.
Her loving husband joined in,
Taking time from the din,
For the world was in need
Of a Christmas cookie.

And then those cookies flew
To the homeless in view,
To a boy whose eyes lit
Like the sparkling star
On Christ's birthday afar.
Celebrations begin
With a Christmas cookie.

Then a tiny, sweet girl
In a voice small and frail,
Five or six years of age,
Came to God's center stage,
Peeking into the box
For a Christmas cookie.

"May I have one," she said,
"For my little sister?"

That's when God's love became
A Christmas cookie.

NAOMI TERRANELLA

A High School Teacher's Prayer

Precious children playing thugs:
Knives, guns, booze, and evil drugs.

How shall I forgive them?
Jesus states in brevity:
Forgive your brothers seventy times seventy.[1]

What do I offer in place of guns and dope?
Jesus says it's simple. Give them love and hope.

Tell them that the blind shall see,
The lame shall walk,
The deaf shall hear[2]
For so much more than one school year,
And make it clear: life begins without fear.

Precious children playing thugs:
Knives, guns, booze, and evil drugs.

What can I teach them?
How do I reach them?
What words will change them
And let them know they count?

How about the Bible's words,
"The Sermon on the Mount."

NAOMI TERRANELLA

---

[1] Matthew 18:22
[2] Matthew 11:5

The Sermon on the Mount

BLESSED ARE THE POOR IN SPIRIT:
FOR THEIRS IS THE KINGDOM OF HEAVEN.

BLESSED ARE THOSE WHO MOURN:
FOR THEY SHALL BE COMFORTED.

BLESSED ARE THE MEEK:
FOR THEY SHALL INHERIT THE EARTH.

BLESSED ARE THEY WHO HUNGER
AND THIRST AFTER RIGHTEOUSNESS:
FOR THEY SHALL BE FILLED.

BLESSED ARE THE MERCIFUL:
FOR THEY SHALL OBTAIN MERCY.

BLESSED ARE THE PURE IN HEART:
FOR THEY SHALL SEE GOD.

BLESSED ARE THE PEACEMAKERS:
FOR THEY SHALL BE CALLED SONS OF GOD.

BLESSED ARE THOSE WHO ARE PERSECUTED
FOR RIGHTEOUSNESS' SAKE,
FOR THEIRS IS THE KINGDOM OF HEAVEN.

JESUS CHRIST,
AS QUOTED IN
MATTHEW 5:3–10

A Letter to Fear

You listen, Fear,
Get outta here!
Our God is near.

We've conquered death.
With our very last breath,
We will praise God's name.
You'll be sorry you came.

Heaven's light will shine,
No more hate and crime.
We'll rejoice with love.
We have Heaven above.

We'll hold each other,
Sister and brother.
If you think Fear will win,
Think again.

NAOMI TERRANELLA

**FOR GOD HAS NOT GIVEN US A SPIRIT
OF FEAR, BUT OF POWER AND OF LOVE
AND OF A SOUND MIND.**

2 TIMOTHY 1:7

SING TO THE LORD WITH THANKSGIVING;
SING PRAISES ON THE HARP TO OUR GOD,
WHO COVERS THE EARTH WITH CLOUDS, WHO
PREPARES RAIN FOR THE EARTH, WHO MAKES
GRASS GROW ON THE MOUNTAINS.

PSALM 147:7–8

A Mountain Walk

Forgiving, accepting, You answered my prayer.
There is love in the air everywhere.

The flowers are singing Your name as they bloom.
The squirrels chirp in laughter; the birds wave a plume.
The rocks at my feet tell how solid You are,
And it's comforting to know You're not far.

Oh, Father, I thank You for the joy that You bring
When I see everything through Your will:

Your flowers, Your creatures, Your pleasures to sing,
And Your gift of the cross on the hill.

Forgiving, accepting, You answered my prayer.
There is love in the air everywhere.

Oh, Father, I thank You for the Son that You gave,
To be worthy of Your love, to be saved.

NAOMI TERRANELLA

A Wheelchair

I see you sitting in a wheelchair,
Wondering how and why you are there.
A tear rolls from your eye.

You're gonna walk. You're gonna fly.
You're gonna know the reason why
God created you, a chosen few,
To reveal Himself through you.

God is holding you.
He will pull you through,
Someday, through His Heaven's door.
Heaven's worth waiting for.

And He'll wipe the tears from your eyes.
There will be no more pain, no more sorrow.[3]
Look forward to God's tomorrow
When He'll make, for you, all things new.

Right now, believe, have faith. He'll hold you,
And all your hopes and dreams will come true.
He's here, right by your side.
Remember, Heaven is forevermore.
And when you, finally, walk through God's door.
He'll smile, and you'll no longer cry.

You're gonna walk. You're gonna fly.
You're gonna know the reason why
God created you, a chosen few,
To reveal Himself to you.

NAOMI TERRANELLA

**THOSE WHO WAIT ON THE LORD SHALL RENEW
THEIR STRENGTH; THEY SHALL RUN AND NOT
BE WEARY, THEY SHALL WALK AND NOT FAINT.**

ISAIAH 40:31

---

[3] Revelation 21:4

All Things a Toy

A day in the life of an active child,
Who's pretending at play, tends to run wild.

When launching their spaceship,
They count down from ten.
Their trip takes them further
When shared with a friend.

They can make of nothing
A fifteen-course meal,
Then wash all the dishes
As part of the deal.

Whether fighting a giant,
Or driving a car,
With them, there's no limit
How big or how far.

Their sandbox an ocean,
'Neath their jungle gym ship,
Energy in motion,
Boundless their trip.

All things a toy,
Laughs, leaps, and giggles,
And when they're excited,
Everything wiggles.

To ponder the world
Through their loving view
Is God's gift from Heaven
For me and for you.

RONALD TERRANELLA

Psalm 95
Come let us sing
For joy to the Lord;
Let us shout aloud to the
Rock of our salvation,
Let us come before Him
With thanksgiving
And extol Him with
Music and song

All Time Divine

Let us give thanks to You, Holy One,
As we marvel at things You have done.
The work of Your hands
Seen in bountiful lands,
In Your oceans, and heavenly sun.

In all the earth, all the stars, and all time,
There is nothing as ever so divine
As our God, Holy God.

In Your Word, all Your glory and majesty,
Everything that can set a heart free.
In Your grace, gentleness,
In Your peace, healing rest,
In Your joy, that You give willingly,

In all the earth, all the stars, and all time,
There is nothing as ever so divine,
As our God, Holy God.

Our God gives us hope for tomorrow,
Love that fills our lives from within,
Shelter in the midst of our sorrow,
And a heart to worship Him.

NAOMI TERRANELLA

THE HEAVENS DECLARE THE GLORY OF GOD, AND THE FIRMAMENT SHOWS HIS HANDIWORK.

PSALM 19:1

An Old Irish Prayer

I heard an old Irish prayer
(I just don't know who wrote it,)
And I want to sing to You
To tell You I'm devoted.

The prayer that I hear
Singing in my ear
Goes like this:

"May the rest of your life
Be the best of your life."

What a wonderful thought I hear!
And the joy that You give
Helps me learn how to live.
Father, teach me, reach me with this prayer.

"May the rest of your life
Be the best of your life."

Father, thank You, for I know I'm in Your care.

NAOMI TERRANELLA

PSALM 66:3

Awesome

"Awesome" is a vibrant word
That's overused by far,
For a woman's hair color
Or for a brand-new car.

But stand beside a turbulent sea
Beneath a harvest moon,
Or watch a cheetah running,
Or see a flying loon.

Technology is something else,
And all that will ensue,
But I'm reserving "awesome", Lord,
For all that's done by You.

DONALD TERRANELLA

FOR BY GRACE, YOU HAVE BEEN SAVED THROUGH FAITH, AND NOT BY YOURSELVES; IT IS THE GIFT OF GOD.

EPHESIANS 2:8

Back to You

At times, being a Christian becomes very hard.
I find myself sneaking out of heaven's yard,
Into the world, as if I'd been hurled by my will.

Oh no!

But You come and find
My soul when I'm blind,
And lead me back to You.

Back to You, where You love me.
Back to You, far above me,
And I'm glad, once again,
To behold You, my Friend
As You welcome me
Back to You.

How can I explain the grace You offer me?
As the sand is comforted by the cooling sea,
As the earth is cleansed by the gentle rain,
My faithful Friend, You lead me back again.

You come and find
My soul when I'm blind
And lead me back to You.

NAOMI TERRANELLA

**IN HIM WE HAVE REDEMPTION THROUGH
HIS BLOOD, THE FORGIVENESS OF SINS,
ACCORDING TO THE RICHES OF HIS GRACE.**

EPHESIANS 1:7

Because of My Sin
(Luke 23 1–56)

I love You, Lord, for all You've done,
And more for who You are:
The Lord of Lords, the King of Kings,
The Lamb born 'neath the star.

Your peace passes all understanding.
Your Spirit gives life to the dead.
You've given the gift of salvation
Through the cleansing blood You've shed.

You've taken my beatings upon You
And the stripes that were meant for me.
You paid for my crimes, so that I might live.
Through Your suffering, set me free.

To the cross You were nailed, though innocent,
Through hands that held no blame.
The crown of thorns was meant for me,
But You wore them to cover my shame.

And still, as You hung there dying,
You selflessly saved one more soul,
Inviting the thief into paradise,
And restoring the broken to whole.

And then You said, "Father, forgive them
For they know not what they do."
Because of my sin, You were nailed to that tree.
The price for my soul was You.

To lay down one's life, there is no greater love
That a person could show to a friend,
But to die such a death for your enemies,
Shows the perfect affection You send.

As a man, You have said, "I love you."
But as God, You have shown beyond doubt.
So how, when my eyes have been opened,
Could I pass through life leaving You out?

You've given more than I have coming
For all I deserve is death.
You gave up Your life to pay for my sin,
And forgiven with Your dying breath.

So, Lord, how could I ever thank You
For all You've done for me?
For bearing the load that I could not bear
On the cross at Calvary.

RONALD TERRANELLA

Becoming Whole

Good will grow from tainted seed
With much fruit on my branches.
Your cattle on a thousand hills
Would wander toward my ranches.

My hope would not be hope deferred
But hope to live forever.
Like Joseph, I'd receive the coat
Of favor in foul weather.

My journeys all would profit
And all would end in peace.
And, finally, enmity with God,
And war with You would cease.

My ends could be beginnings
And those beginnings never end.
Then, I would never be alone
For You would be my friend.

And I'd be safe forever, even if I die.
For death, in life, with Jesus
Leads on to a brighter sky.

Who can compare the years we live
With all the years in time?
Where Heaven is, there is no fear,
No lust, deceit, or crime.

A place of perfect worship
Before the sovereign God,
Whose every word is wonderful.
All saints and hosts applaud.

And there in Heaven, as on Earth,
You only give good things;
Like joy, peace, love, and honor
That belief in Your Son brings.

With the Creator of all things,
We're granted audience
For worship and to supplicate
In all our needs and wants.

All that I have to give to You,
In exchange for all You give,
Is my humble thanks and worship
And hope that I might live.

I thank you, Lord, for hearing
My plead from this mortal soul,
And giving me Your healing love
And chance to become whole.

RONALD TERRANELLA

Behold

BEHOLD, I STAND AT THE DOOR AND KNOCK
IF ANYONE HEARS MY VOICE, AND OPENS THE
DOOR, I WILL COME IN . . .

REVELATION 3:20

Forgiving my sin?
Should I let grace abound, now that I'm found,
And You've given this peace to me?
Should I let grace abound, now that I'm found,
And Your truth has set me free?

CERTAINLY NOT! HOW SHALL WE WHO DIED TO
SIN LIVE ANY LONGER IN IT?

ROMANS 6:2

I behold the life You offer me
In Your Word, the perfect plan.
I behold You God Almighty,
Great I Am, the Son of Man.

In Your joy, Your stars, Your oceans
As You hold me in Your hand.
I behold You, Lord, Messiah,
Prince of Peace since time began.

He who has an ear to listen,
He who has an eye to behold,

He who has a heart to feel
Let it be told, let it be bold:
You've opened His door.
You're searching no more.
You have found God's chosen Son.
Behold. Your life has begun.

NAOMI TERRANELLA

HE WHO HAS AN EAR TO LISTEN, LET HIM HEAR
WHAT THE SPIRIT SAYS TO THE CHURCHES.

REVELATION 2:11

BEHOLD WHAT MANNER OF LOVE THE FATHER
HAS BESTOWED ON US, THAT WE SHOULD BE
CALLED CHILDREN OF GOD.

JOHN 3:1

Bliss

I have a lot of love in my heart.
Here I am, trying to practice the art
Of poetry You give to me
To serve You, and You know it.
So, please, God, help me show it:
That love You give that lets me live
In bliss that not a soul should miss.

NAOMI TERRANELLA

Books My Name Wasn't In

I used to do evil and hated all good.
I took what I wanted whenever I could.
I'd fill my desires and did what I'd say.
It just doesn't matter who gets hurt today.

Sometimes I'd get caught up and take any dare.
Then things might get shot up. I just didn't care.
My homeboys were wicked. Our women were wild.
I was only a teen, but don't call me a child.

I got on the dope. I'd rob, steal, and kill.
I'd unload my magnum for a ten-dollar bill.
My hood was the greatest, all my friends thugs.
I'd keep up on the latest with drinking and drugs.

Just hope that you're welcome if you come to my street,
Or I'll give you a pounding; then you'd better beat feet.
One day I stepped out, and the enemy caught me.
Though ducking and dodging, the other guy shot me.

I dropped like a stone. The sky had grown dark.
Out went the lights as I died in the park,
But soon I was conscious in a hot and dark place.
I was stricken with horror when I saw my host's face.

Satan was laughing as I stood there bleeding.
Twisted and gruesome was the crew he was leading.
He said, "Good to see you, my son. You've done well.
You've been a good soldier, now welcome to Hell!"

I was proud of you, son, when you punched-out your teacher
And happier still when you spit on the preacher.
You lived like I wanted your whole life for me.
So now, I'll reward you as you will soon see.

Then he pinned me with hooks that dug in my skin
And opened some books that my name wasn't in.
He told me, "It's over. You now have no hope.
You've forsaken your Savior for violence and dope."

"You've lived like a heathen, and so here you'll stay.
You've missed-out on mercy. It's too late to pray!"
Then he threw me in fire secured by a chain,
And said, "You are dead now, but will not be slain!"

Then my eyes had gone dim, and my skin started burning.
The pain was so great; for death I was yearning.
The flames were so hot that I couldn't shed tears.
The worst part: forever's not measured in years.

RONALD TERRANELLA

BUT THE LORD IS FAITHFUL, WHO WILL
ESTABLISH YOU AND GUARD YOU FROM THE
EVIL ONE,
AND WE HAVE CONFIDENCE IN THE LORD
CONCERNING YOU, BOTH THAT YOU DO AND
WILL DO THE THINGS THAT WE COMMAND
YOU.
NOW, MAY THE LORD DIRECT YOUR HEARTS
INTO THE LOVE OF GOD AND INTO THE
PATIENCE OF CHRIST.

THESSALONIANS 3:3–5

HAVE MERCY UPON ME, O GOD. ACCORDING TO
YOUR LOVINGKINDNESS; ACCORDING TO THE
MULTITUDE OF YOUR TENDER MERCIES.

BLOT OUT MY TRANSGRESSIONS. WASH ME
THOROUGHLY FROM MY INIQUITY,
AND CLEANSE ME FROM MY SIN.

PSALM 51:1–2

Brainwashed

I've been brainwashed,
Washed of my sin.
God is my redeemer.
I want to live for Him.

Take your worldly stuff.
I've had enough.
Sin no longer rules me.
I'm focused on eternity.

I've been brainwashed,
Washed of my sin.
Now that I'm believing,
God has welcomed me in.

NAOMI TERRANELLA

Chance

Chance is the path in life we take
That can lead us to love
Or our hearts to break.

To brighten your future
Or darken your past,
Lead you to torture
Or bliss that will last.

Chance is a demon,
Chance is a saint,
A black, clouded evening
Or a rainbow to paint.

Our dreams to come true
Or efforts to fail,
Fill our skies with blue
Or cause us to wail.

Fate is a road
That is paved by chance,
Weighed down by our load
Or enlightened to dance.

Our trails are uncertain.
The future is dim.
I thank God for the chance
That led me to Him.

RONALD TERRANELLA

**BEAR ONE ANOTHER'S BURDENS, AND SO
FULFILL THE LAW OF CHRIST.**

GALATIANS 6:2

Chaos

God, I'm trying to be
What You want me to be,
But the chaos around me
Is all that I see.
People needing me here, there,
And everywhere.
I want to show them
That I know them
And that I truly care.

So, You tell me, don't worry.
Hear only Your commands.
You've got it. You're on it.
Got the world in Your hands.

NAOMI TERRANELLA

**AND LET US NOT GROW WEARY WHILE DOING
GOOD, FOR IN DUE SEASON WE SHALL REAP IF
WE DO NOT LOSE HEART.**

**THEREFORE, AS WE HAVE OPPORTUNITY, LET US
DO GOOD TO ALL, ESPECIALLY TO THOSE WHO
ARE OF THE HOUSEHOLD OF FAITH.**

GALATIANS 6:9–10

COME TO ME, ALL YOU WHO LABOR AND ARE
HEAVY LADEN, AND I WILL GIVE YOU REST. TAKE
MY YOKE UPON YOU AND LEARN OF ME, FOR I
AM GENTLE AND LOWLY IN HEART, AND YOU
WILL FIND REST FOR YOUR SOULS.

FOR MY YOKE IS EASY,
AND MY BURDEN IS LIGHT.

MATTHEW 11:28–30

Come To Me

I fall to Your throne—weary and worn—
Feeling alone.
And here, in Your control,
I find a peace restoring my soul.
You're lifting the veil, taking weakness and shame.
I'm hearing Your voice, softly calling my name.
I hear, "Come all you burdened and weary,
And I will give you rest,
Lay your head upon My chest.
I will carry you, hold you, and comfort you
Making you whole,
And you will find rest for your soul."[4]
"Take My yoke upon you, learn of Me,
And I'll value your heart.
Take My hand, and your blessings will start.
For My yoke is easy, and My burden is light.
I'll embrace you with peaceful delight."[5]
I rest—finally found—here in Your arms,
Burdens laid down.
Your peace, comforting me, filling my heart,
Setting me free.

"Come to Me for I offer true rest.
Lay your head upon My chest."

NAOMI TERRANELLA

---

[4] Matthew 11:28
[5] Matthew 11:29

Dancing with You

The clock struck twelve.
Prince Charming never came.
You never gave me winks, or wealth,
Or beauty pageant fame.

But You fill my heart
With joy beyond belief,
And You have made me sing
Through sorrow and through grief.

So, I'm dancing with You.
How wonderful is this?
I'm dancing with You.
I'm in ballerina bliss.

I take Your hand.
You turn me around.
When my steps get lost,
I pray and then I'm found.

I'm dancing with You.

NAOMI TERRANELLA

Dear Moon

Lonesome Moon, ancient orb,
Mysterious is your gaze.
Your autumn emerald opaque rings
Prewarn of rain filled days.

Silent vigil from shadows peek
On some nights all together hid.
Minor prints of visits few
To valiant men farewell you bid.

Never do you turn away,
Your back exposed to endless space.
In days of old the pagans pray
To warrant bliss from frozen face.

Anticipated tidings shine
On mystics so itinerate.
Their guesses often self-fulfilled,
Yet, still adore you in prostrate.

Sorcerers cry and wiccans plead
Unto your light in high esteem.
The Devil's sacrifices bleed
Offered up by evil's meme.

If you could speak, what would you say
Of good and evil you have watched,
From abominations of the fiend,
To lovers as they touched?
You were made just days before
God's spirit was to Adam breathed.
You watched man's fall and saw the flood,
Then, hope as Jesus teethed.

You looked in silence at man's fall,
His pleasures, peace, and war.
Through time, have given life to fear
From tales 'round fire's lore.

Oh, Luna, shining clod of dust,
Blamed for maddened fits of lust,
Always faithful dimpled crust,
In guilt I stand before.

RONALD TERRANELLA

**PURE AND UNDEFILED RELIGION BEFORE GOD
AND THE FATHER IS THIS: TO VISIT ORPHANS
AND WIDOWS IN THEIR TROUBLE, AND TO
KEEP ONESELF UNSPOTTED FROM THE WORLD.**

JAMES 1:27

Dear Orphan

Jesus said
That His people love you, orphan.
Jesus said
That His church will love you too.
Jesus said
That He will not leave you orphaned.
He will shelter and comfort you.

For our Father's true religion
Sends you hands to comfort you.
He has formed you, and He loves you,
And He tells us what to do.

Peace, be still.
You are in God's will.
His promises still stand.
Take hold of His hand.

NAOMI TERRANELLA

**I WILL NOT LEAVE YOU ORPHANS; I WILL COME TO YOU.
JOHN 14:18**

GOD RESISTS THE PROUD,
BUT GIVES GRACE TO THE HUMBLE.

PROVERBS 3:34

THEREFORE, HUMBLE YOURSELVES UNDER THE
MIGHTY HAND OF GOD, THAT HE MIGHT EXALT
YOU IN DUE TIME, CASTING ALL YOUR CARES
UPON HIM, FOR HE CARES FOR YOU.

1 PETER. 5:6

Decisions of Submission

Decisions of submission,
Father, hold us in Your will.
Your glory surrounds us
Sea to sea, valley to hill.

Teach us how to know You
For we really want to,
And our cups You'll overfill.
Decisions of submission,
Father, tell us "Peace, be still."[6]

Hold us today and all through the night.
Cast our cares away. Grant us peace
And strength through Your might.

---

[6] Mark 4:39

Decisions of submission,
Father, help us do Your will.
We pray to give You honor
Sea to sea, valley to hill.

NAOMI TERRANELLA

DAVID DANCED BEFORE THE LORD WITH ALL HIS MIGHT.

2 SAMUEL 6:14

E-Motion

The joy of the dance, an artist in motion,
Inspires romance like a wave on the ocean.

To bare your own soul, expressed in your fashion,
And to become whole fueled by your passion.

To convey a story, without any words,
Can fulfill your soul as flight does to birds.

Your styles, your brush stroke, music the beat,
A moth drawn to fire, enticed by the heat,

A music box icon, a fairy, the swan,
Still waters, a cyclone, closed lilies at dawn.

Though the steps are the same,
Each performance a sequel,
A flickering flame, ablaze with no equal,

To float like a feather, aloft on the breeze,
Your heart's engine racing,
The song holds the keys.

Exhausting excitement, all that you can be,
For only when dancing is your spirit set free.

RONALD TERRANELLA

Eternity

I stumbled through this world,
Without You, on a starless night;
Then, I saw Your light shine through.
What a glorious sight!

No direction in my life.
I walked a circular path.
No redemption, only strife,
Called for God's great wrath.

From the darkness, I reached out
And grasped at something I couldn't view.
As Your mercy pulled me out,
I now could see that it was You.

Thank you, Lord, for loving me.
I can't believe You believe in me.
I'll live for You. You died for me;
So, we can share eternity.

You picked me up, dusted me clean,
And taught me ways to follow You.
And for the strength to carry on,
My undying love and gratitude.

Wish there was something I could do
To prove how much You mean to me.
I can only give You thanks and praise,
Yet You return eternity.

DONALD TERRANELLA

NOW MAY THE LORD DIRECT YOUR HEARTS
INTO THE LOVE OF GOD AND INTO THE
PATIENCE OF CHRIST.

2 THESSALONIANS 3:5

Five Smooth Stones

For forty days he taunted
The army of the Lord,
And forty nights he haunted
God's people with his sword.

But lo' there came a child
To bring his brothers' lunch;
He spied mighty Goliath,
The titan, and his bunch.

Who will fight this giant
And still his angry tones?
I will take him down, he thought,
With God and five smooth stones.

How could this child face this man
Who'd battled since his youth?
He stood at almost nine foot ten,
But David knew the truth.

The Lord would not forsake him
While facing such poor odds.
His faith said he could take him.
The victory was God's.

There David stood, with sling in hand,
The outcome seeming dark.
Goliath fell and shook the land.
The missile met its mark.

The battle's toll; one giant dead;
A promise kept; he took his head.
Philistia's army turned and fled
From God and five smooth stones.[7]

RONALD TERRANELLA

[7] 1 Samuel 17:1–58

God's Birthday Child

You are God's birthday child.
Sing His praise and sing it loud.

Birthdays will come.
Birthdays will go.
Time will move fast.
Time will move slow.

But since you know
God, who loves you,
Your light will glow
When candles are through.

With God you stand
Cupped in His hand,
Sheltered from harms,
Wrapped in His arms.

You are His birthday child.
Feel His love. You make Him proud.

NAOMI TERRANELLA

O LORD, HOW GREAT ARE YOUR WORKS!

PSALM 92:5

God's Face

God has a face that's pure and clean.
No finer face a man has seen.

It shines down from the skies above.
The heavens touch our hearts with love.

It grows up from the earth of green
And every corner in between.

It spouts up from the ocean blue
And beautifies the desert too.

God's face is clear for all to see.
I give God thanks for showing me.

RONALD TERRANELLA

**O DEATH, WHERE IS THY STING? O GRAVE,
WHERE IS THY VICTORY?**

1 CORINTHIANS 15:55

God's Glory Shines Through

Beauty for ashes, God's glory shines through.
Life everlasting, His children renewed.

Peace in His heaven, peace pulls us through.
Beauty for ashes, God's glory shines through.

He takes the fears, ends all the tears,
Breaks through the core of the terrors of war.

Righteousness and praise,
Glowing peace through the haze.

Beauty for ashes, God's glory shines through.

Hear a choir of angels sing
As the souls in flight take wing.

Beauty for ashes, God's glory shines through.[8]

NAOMI TERRANELLA

---
[8] 1 Corinthians 15:55

God's Hands

My God's hands are full of wonders.
They guide me round life's foolish blunders.

They catch my arm if I should stumble,
Then break my fall the times I tumble.

They dust me off, and mark the trail
That I should follow without fail.
Then His hands hold me, though undeserving,
They shape and mold me 'till I am serving.

They lift me up and make me whole,
Then smooth the wrinkles from my soul.

RONALD TERRANELLA

BEHOLD WHAT MANNER OF LOVE THE FATHER
HAS BESTOWED ON US, THAT WE SHOULD BE
CALLED THE CHILDREN OF GOD!

1 JOHN 3:1

God's Retirement Plan

I've lived through grace
And have been approved
To meet the Son of Man,
And now it's time to reap the perks
Of God's retirement plan.

My monthly check is made out to
"A Child of God," myself.
The amount that it is written for
Is all of Heaven's wealth.

The community I live in
Is gated all around.
In the morning, I'm awakened
By the singing angels' sound.

I've never seen a pothole here
For the streets are paved with gold.
The doors are made of giant pearls,
A wonder to behold.

The light all around this mansion shines
Of glory, day by day,
The man next door is Jesus,
And God lives down the way.

The health plan is the best I've seen
For my body is brand new,
One that will last forever
With no down payment due.

The park is just around the bend
Where the grass is green, and water still.
A table is set to picnic at
Though my cup always seems to spill.

Layered jewels construct the walls
And gems provide the tiles.
You've never seen such giant halls.
They're fifteen thousand miles.

Mere words cannot describe this place
For things are here I'd never seen:
The Shekinah glory of God's hands,
Even the trash, pristine.

Saint Peter is the doorman,
A fairly cheerful dude,
But those he's told to turn away,
Well, they get pretty rude.

The finest things the world can give
Are worse than Heaven's junk.
Earth's treasures are but refuse here,
Its fragrant scents are funk.

Be careful with your choices
For they decide your end:
Take heed to evil voices?
Or, let Jesus be your friend?

Be ready to come up here
When you hear the trumpets sound,
For I hear conditions aren't so great
In that crowded place "down" town.

RONALD TERRANELLA

I WILL SING OF THE MERCIES OF THE LORD
FOREVER; WITH MY MOUTH WILL MAKE
KNOWN YOUR FAITHFULNESS TO ALL
GENERATIONS.

PSALM 89:1

God, Mercy and Love

God, mercy and love.
God, strength from above.
You feel my despair,
Then, You take me where
Clouds fall to Your love:
To Your rainbows above.

Lord, with Your embrace,
Give redeeming grace.
You, when I am torn,
Take hold of the thorn.
Then, Your Son I've found,
Whom You chose
To wear Your crown.

NAOMI TERRANELLA

Heaven's Realm

Dear Father God, You are the One
Who makes my life worth living,
For how could I bear all my sin
Without Your kind forgiving?

Without Your grace and mercy,
How could I clean my slate,
And what would my life be like
With a mind that's reprobate?

What kind of love would I have
If all I loved was dark?
I'd soon be dry and withered,
Like a tree stripped of its bark.

For where is life, if all my plans,
Lead only to the grave?
My light would be a moonless night
At midnight in a cave.

Would I find joy in hatred
As one who hates all joy?
And how could I advance my ranks
With nothing to deploy?

If all my life is moving toward
A future that's my end,
And, after that, the fiery pit
Is just around the bend;

Then where could I find meaning
If everything meant not?
Could I accomplish anything,
And if I could then what?

If no good came from nothing,
And everything was bad;
Then where would be my happiness
If everything was sad?

Where could the hope of hope be
If all hope would be lost?
Where would the clean of soap be
If nothing could be washed?

Is anything worth having
If nothing could be kept;
If under my life's carpet,
All good things had been swept?

If legacies end when I do,
And all my going ceases,
The destiny of all I've done
Is to be dashed to pieces.

I could not even wonder,
At a time, if I was saved,
As every thought grows sicker,
My best is but depraved.

What would tomorrow be like
If the next day was just worse,
If my first ride in a limo
Is my last ride in a hearse?

But, with You in my life, dear God,
As Captain at the helm,
Every turn You make with me
Leads on to Heaven's Realm.

RONALD TERRANELLA

ONE GENERATION SHALL PRAISE YOUR WORKS
TO ANOTHER AND SHALL DECLARE YOUR
MIGHTY ACTS. I WILL MEDITATE ON THE
GLORIOUS SPLENDOR OF YOUR MAJESTY, AND
ON YOUR WONDROUS WORKS.

PSALM 145:4–5

Heavenly Sights

(Psalm 8:1–9)

We sense Your glory
In Your marvelous seas.
We feel caresses
In Your soul-healing breeze.
We see Your starlight
Glowing, showing Your might.
You are The Maker
Of all heavenly sights.

We see the baby
Nestled in Daddy's arms.
We see the Mommy
And all of God's charms.
We see the grandson
Wheeling Grandmother's chair.
We sense the angels
Smiling, ruffling his hair.

Heavenly sights, heavenly sights.
You are the Maker
Of all heavenly sights.

We read Your Bible
With Your promise of life.
We feel Your mercy
Through our troubles and strife.
We see the mountains
Lifted up by Your might.
We see Your rainbows:
Sparkling blessings of light.

Heavenly sights, heavenly sights.
You are The Maker
Of all heavenly sights.

We see the eagles
Soaring into Your sky.
We feel Your love flow
Lifting spirits so high.
Your flowing water,
Cleansing all of our sin.
We praise You, Father,
Lord, we thank You again.

Heavenly sights, heavenly sights.
You are The Maker
Of all heavenly sights.

NAOMI TERRANELLA

WHERE CAN I GO FROM YOUR SPIRIT?
OR WHERE CAN I FLEE FROM YOUR PRESENCE?

IF I ASCEND INTO HEAVEN, YOU ARE THERE;
IF I MAKE MY BED IN HELL, BEHOLD, YOU
ARE THERE.

IF I TAKE THE WINGS OF THE MORNING, AND
DWELL IN THE UTTERMOST PARTS OF THE SEA,
EVEN THERE YOUR HAND SHALL LEAD ME, AND
YOUR RIGHT HAND SHALL HOLD ME

PSALM 139: 7–10

Hide and Seek

Father, Abba, here I am
Playing hide and seek again.
I try to hide, but You search for me.
How can I show You
Things no one wants to see?
How can I tell You that I'm so sorry?

I need to find a hiding place,
Running from Your love and healing grace.
You know my secrets, know my shame,
But still, I hear You call my name.
Telling me to run home free.
Father, Abba, come and find me.

As I run from You,
You search for me,
Longing to set me free
To offer me eternity.

Father, Abba, I'm tired of playing hide & seek.
I feel my heart grow cold and weak.
I can't even hear You speak.

Father, Abba, It's dark in this hiding place.
I need to feel Your love and grace.
I want to feel Your warm embrace.

Then, I run home to Your love
That captures me, and suddenly
You set me free.
You rescue me from me.

This game You've won:
Thy will be done.

NAOMI TERRANELLA

**HE ALONE IS MY REFUGE AND MY FORTRESS;
MY GOD, IN HIM I WILL TRUST.**

PSALM 91:2

THEN JESUS CRIED OUT AND SAID, HE WHO
BELIEVES IN ME, BELIEVES NOT IN ME, BUT IN
HIM WHO SENT ME.

AND HE WHO SEES ME SEES HIM WHO SENT ME.

I HAVE COME AS A LIGHT INTO THE WORLD,
THAT WHOEVER BELIEVES IN ME SHOULD NOT
ABIDE IN DARKNESS.

JOHN 12:44–46

Hill of Light

Shattered glass, broken dreams,
Life is bursting at the seams.
All I know, want to go
To that home in Bible dreams.
Where is the caring? Where is the love?
I lift my heart to God above.

And He takes me to the hill of light.
Heaven's in my sight.
Where Jesus died for me on Calvary
To the hill of light.

I see you standing there
Thinking there's no one to care.
Come with me, take my hand,
Let's go to the promised land:

There is the caring. There is the love.
We'll lift our hearts to His Heaven above.
And He'll take us to the hill of light.
Heaven's in our sight.
Where Jesus set us free on Calvary
To the hill of light.

NAOMI TERRANELLA

AND GOD WILL WIPE AWAY EVERY TEAR FROM
THEIR EYES; THERE SHALL BE NO MORE DEATH,
NOR SORROW, NOR CRYING; AND THERE SHALL
BE NO MORE PAIN, FOR THE FORMER THINGS
HAVE PASSED AWAY.

REVELATION 21:4

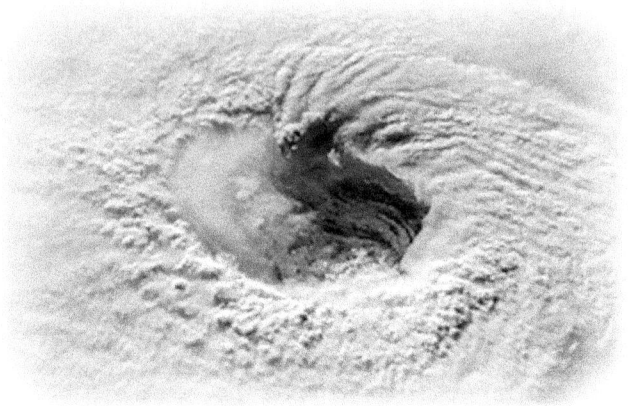

Hurricane

We do not want you
To visit our town.
Get out of here!
We don't want you around.
You came uninvited,
Wherever you went,
And left in your wake
Despair and lament.

Bold and obtrusive,
And drinking your fill,
We've already seen that
You're willing to kill.
Your wind and your rain,
Incredible souse,
Left the strongest of men
Boarded up in their house.

Much smarter than us,
As you launch your attack,
You faked to the East,
Like a cool running back.
Then you ran to the West,
So that some would be spared,
And trained your attention
On those less prepared.

You Ironically lingered
Destroying our brethren.
We pray that your victims
Were sent-off to Heaven.
Like your twisters before you,
You then disappeared.
Guess what! We've got God,
So, there's nothing to fear.

DONALD TERRANELLA

FOR YOU HAVE BEEN A STRENGTH TO THE
POOR, A STRENGTH TO THE NEEDY IN HIS
DISTRESS, A REFUGE FROM THE STORM.

ISAIAH 25:4

THEREFORE, I SAY TO YOU, DO NOT WORRY
ABOUT YOUR LIFE, WHAT YOU WILL EAT OR
DRINK; NOR ABOUT YOUR BODY, WHAT YOU
WILL PUT ON IT. IS NOT LIFE MORE THAN FOOD
AND THE BODY MORE THAN CLOTHING?

LOOK AT THE BIRDS OF THE AIR, FOR THEY
NEITHER SOW NOR REAP NOR GATHER INTO
BARNS; YET YOUR HEAVENLY FATHER FEEDS
THEM. ARE YOU NOT OF MORE VALUE THAN
THEY?

WHICH OF YOU BY WORRYING CAN ADD ONE
CUBIT TO HIS STATURE?

SO, WHY WORRY ABOUT CLOTHING? CONSIDER
THE LILIES OF THE FIELD, HOW THEY GROW; THEY
NEITHER TOIL OR SPIN; AND YET, I SAY TO YOU
THAT EVEN SOLOMON IN ALL HIS GLORY WAS NOT
ARRAYED LIKE ONE OF THESE.

MATTHEW 6:25–29

THE LORD EXECUTES RIGHTEOUSNESS AND
JUSTICE FOR ALL WHO ARE OPPRESSED. HE
MADE KNOWN HIS WAYS TO MOSES, HIS ACTS
TO THE CHILDREN OF ISRAEL. THE LORD IS
MERCIFUL AND GRACIOUS, SLOW TO ANGER,
AND ABOUNDING IN MERCY.

HE WILL NOT ALWAYS STRIVE WITH US. NOR
WILL HE KEEP HIS ANGER FOREVER. HE HAS
NOT DEALT WITH US ACCORDING TO OUR SINS.
NOR PUNISHED US ACCORDING TO OUR
INIQUITIES. FOR THE HEAVENS ARE HIGH
ABOVE THE EARTH.

SO GREAT IS HIS MERCY TOWARD THOSE
WHO FEAR HIM: AS FAR AS THE EAST IS FROM
THE WEST, SO FAR HAS HE REMOVED OUR
TRANSGRESSIONS FROM US.

AS A FATHER PITIES HIS CHILDREN, SO THE
LORD PITIES THOSE WHO FEAR HIM.

PSALM 103:6–13

I Will Give You Rest

He said come to Me,
And I will give you rest,[9]
And your sins will be as far from you
As East is from the West.[10]

As a flower on a barren ground
Can turn my soul around,
The sound of Your love
Comes from above;
And once again, I'm found.

Lord, we never know the treasures
You have waiting around the bend.
When sadness tries to hold me down,
You're there. You send a friend.

NAOMI TERRANELLA

---

[9] Matthew 11:28
[10] Psalm 103:11–12

I'll Meet You There

Someday, when my life is through,
I know I'll finally see You.
God's Word, God's promises are true.

I'll meet You there. I'll meet You there.

Fly over the mountain tops,
Way beyond the eagles.
There will be no looking back.
Wave goodbye to weasels.
Higher than the highest peak
Painted on God's easels.

I'll meet You there. I'll meet You there.

NAOMI TERRANELLA

AND THERE SHALL BE NO NIGHT THERE; THEY
NEED NO LAMP NOR LIGHT OF THE SUN, FOR
THE LORD GOD GIVES THEM LIGHT, AND THEY
SHALL REIGN FOREVER AND EVER.

REVELATION 22:5

THEY SHALL NEITHER HUNGER ANYMORE NOR
THIRST ANYMORE. THE SUN SHALL NOT STRIKE
THEM OR ANY HEAT; FOR THE LAMB WHO IS IN
THE MIDST OF THE THRONE WILL SHEPHERD
THEM AND LEAD THEM TO LIVING FOUNTAINS OF
WATERS, AND GOD WILL WIPE AWAY EVERY TEAR
FROM THEIR EYES.

REVELATION 7:16–17

(The Basis of Fellowship with Jesus:)

THIS IS THE MESSAGE WHICH WE HAVE
HEARD FROM HIM AND DECLARE TO YOU:
THAT GOD IS LIGHT AND IN HIM THERE IS NO
DARKNESS AT ALL.

IF WE SAY WE HAVE FELLOWSHIP WITH HIM,
AND WALK IN DARKNESS, WE LIE AND DO NOT
PRACTICE THE TRUTH.

BUT IF WE WALK IN THE LIGHT, AS HE IS IN
THE LIGHT, WE HAVE FELLOWSHIP WITH ONE
ANOTHER, AND THE BLOOD OF JESUS CHRIST,
HIS SON, CLEANSES US FROM ALL SIN.

IF WE SAY WE HAVE NO SIN, WE DECEIVE
OURSELVES, AND THE TRUTH IS NOT IN US.

IF WE CONFESS OUR SINS, HE IS FAITHFUL AND JUST TO FORGIVE US OUR SINS AND TO CLEANSE US FROM ALL UNRIGHTEOUSNESS.

1 JOHN 1:5–9

I'm Forgiven

So many days I've longed to know
My purpose in Your plan.
So many nights I've longed to feel
The power of Your hand.

Holding me, molding me,
Making me Your own,
Then, finally, revealed to me
The things You've always known:

I'm forgiven; I've no reason to hide.
I'm forgiven; and You call me Your bride.
You will never let me be all alone again.
You're here beside me,
My true and faithful Friend.

As I travel the pages of Your Word,
And I ponder the lessons that I've heard,
Trusting what You've taught me,
Clinging to Your love,
Your Word will guide me
To Your shelter above.

NAOMI TERRANELLA

*(Before Jesus was crucified, He prayed in
the Garden of Gethsemane, saying:)*

**FATHER, IF IT IS YOUR WILL, REMOVE THIS CUP
FROM ME; NEVERTHELESS, NOT MY WILL, BUT
YOURS BE DONE.**

LUKE 22:42

In the Garden

Father, I come to this garden
Alone, to hide my tears.
Though I know that You are with me,
I'm sure You feel my fears.

I pray You find me faithful
As I try to do Your will,
But I'm frightened and I'm broken.
Won't You help me climb this hill?

Father, the answer that You send me,
As You lift my heart in prayer,
Gives peace beyond perfection
And erases my despair.

This burden I must bear now,
But Your promises are clear.
Eternity awaits me.
Father, whom then shall I fear?

NAOMI TERRANELLA

Jesus Bells
(A Christmas poem)

Jesus bells, Jesus bells,
Rudolph got away.
Oh, what fun it is to know
That Christ was born today!

Jesus bells, Jesus bells,
Here's His gift to you:
Lots of peace within your heart
To last your whole life through.

NAOMI TERRANELLA

SING PRAISE TO THE LORD, YOU SAINTS OF HIS,
AND GIVE THANKS AT THE REMEMBRANCE OF
HIS HOLY NAME. FOR HIS ANGER IS BUT
FOR A MOMENT, HIS FAVOR IS FOR LIFE.

WEEPING MAY ENDURE FOR A NIGHT, BUT JOY
COMES IN THE MORNING.

PSALM 30:4–5

Joy in the Morning

You give us joy in the morning,
Peace throughout the day,
Blessings in the evening
As You cast our cares away.

You give us shelter in the darkness,
Sleep, then once again,
Joy in the morning
In the love You freely send.

Joy in the morning,
Peace throughout the day.
Evening reflections
As we bow our heads to pray.

And we can dream within Your presence,
Then awake to Your new day.
Joy in the morning,
Peace throughout the day.

Someday, when we're in Heaven
Swimming in Your crystal lakes,
Dancing in Your golden streets,
Swinging on Your pearly gates;
As Your angels are performing,
And we gather at Your throne,
You'll give us joy in the morning,
More than we have ever known.

NAOMI TERRANELLA

KEEP YOUR HEART WITH ALL DILIGENCE, FOR OUT OF IT SPRING THE ISSUES OF LIFE.

PROVERBS 4:23

Keep Me

Oh, Lord, don't give me over
To a mind that's reprobate
That only dwells on worldly things,
Like greed and lust and hate.

A mind that doesn't know You
And has no love for Yours,
That has nowhere to turn to
But to join in Satan's wars.

That doesn't care of Godly truths
And from sin has no defense.
Denying Your miraculous proof
And believing false pretense.

No longer seeking wisdom
But thinking as a fool
With no sense of discernment
Or remorse for being cruel.

Forsaking understanding
For pleasures of the heart,
Giving up on heavenly things,
Defeated from the start.

To build my house on perishing things,
As a house on shifting sand,
Devoid of all peace Jesus brings,
Barred from the promise land.

Take not from me Your spirit
Or incomparable lasting joy.
Make me a jar for glory,
Not one formed to destroy.

Let me not be guilty
Of the one unpardonable sin:
Denying my salvation
And all that You have been.

May I never become unapproved
Or near to being cursed,
Rejecting You through unbelief
And lose my spiritual thirst.

You give Your grace to all who ask
But not to those who refuse.
May I never fall from enlightenment
And thus, my soul to lose.

RONALD TERRANELLA

**IN THE BEGINNING, GOD CREATED THE
HEAVENS AND THE EARTH.**

GENESIS 1:1

Let There Be Light

Does the pigeon possess any wisdom
Or the sparrow hold any degree?
Can they tell us the meaning of life as it is
Or control the powers that be?

Does the eagle ponder creation
Or the raven quantum relief?
Is the double helix ever on seagulls' minds
Or the origin of belief?

And yet they've been given in common
The brain and dynamics to fly,
To be free of the world, of the earth bound,
Suspended on nothing but sky.

Men have, jealously, been inspired
To strive until they knew just how,
With one drop from God's ocean of knowledge,
Man has copied this achievement of fowl.

God has given to us His examples
And the power to recreate.
He gave us the choice between living and death.
Choose life before it's too late.

Although man, in his wisdom, is foolish,
He has never been left without hope.
He's been given, from God, great intelligence
And ample ability to cope.

From this process of thinking and adapting,
Man has conquered the depths of the sea
And stood on the surface of that lonely moon
Who's been 'round before man came to be.

We have figured the weight of the planets
And have measured the distance to some.
To witness these things, and still not believe,
Our hearts must be deaf, blind, and dumb.

The sun that rises each morning
Was not placed so far that we freeze,
And neither has it been set too close.
Don't we realize such wonders as these?

Some people have faith in a theory:
That we came from some prime mortal ooze
And were formed from some random occurrence.
No evidence endorses this ruse.

The missing link will remain missing
Because it doesn't exist,
Yet some men will always keep searching.
In denial of God, they'll insist.

Some powers will try to convince us
That our minds came from nothing, from chance;
That all of Earth's resources that man puts to use
Are from no more than happenstance.

Now, let's try and be realistic.
Without God, could man be formed from dust?
Could the weather cycle nourish the earth
Or could oil be found 'neath its crust?

Would snow be stored on a mountain
To feed rivers when rain is lean?
The same summer that hinders the rain to fall
Melts the snow to keep everything green.

The ocean that is moved by the power,
From the pull of that ominous moon,
Keeps its shores, through the tides, replenished
And piles its cushioning dune.

And the twilight to see in night hours,
Reflected off old Luna's face,
Is directed to relieve total darkness,
And when failing, the stars take its place.

A seed can produce a flower
That will reach to the heavens in praise.
Let us pray before man's final hour
That the truth be unveiled through the haze.

How could there be any division
To dispute what our hearts know is right:
In the beginning, God created Heaven and Earth
To Your truths, Lord, let there be light.

RONALD TERRANELLA

Jesus explained redemption in a parable.

A shepherd had 100 sheep. One of his sheep strayed and got lost. The shepherd left his flock of 99 sheep and went to search for the lost sheep. When the shepherd found the lost sheep, he rejoiced. The shepherd didn't punish the lost sheep. The sheep that was lost was now found. That gave the shepherd joy.

Jesus used this parable to explain how our heavenly Father searches for us when we go astray. God loves us, even when we go astray.

"TAKE HEED THAT YOU DO NOT DESPISE ONE OF THESE LITTLE ONES, FOR I SAY TO YOU THAT IN HEAVEN THEIR ANGELS ALWAYS SEE THE FACE OF MY FATHER WHO IS IN HEAVEN."

"FOR THE SON OF MAN HAS COME TO SAVE THAT WHICH WAS LOST."

"WHAT DO YOU THINK? IF A MAN HAS A HUNDRED SHEEP, AND ONE OF THEM GOES ASTRAY, DOES HE NOT LEAVE THE NINETY-NINE AND GO TO THE MOUNTAINS TO SEEK THE ONE WHO IS STRAYING?"

"AND IF HE SHOULD FIND IT, ASSUREDLY, I SAY TO YOU, HE REJOICES MORE OVER THAT SHEEP THAN OVER THE NINETY-NINE THAT DID NOT GO ASTRAY."

"EVEN SO IT IS NOT THE WILL OF YOUR FATHER WHO IS IN HEAVEN THAT ONE OF THESE LITTLE ONES SHOULD PERISH."

MATTHEW 18:10–14

Lost Sheep are Loved

Holy Spirit, please seek me
I've lost my way.
Holy Shepherd, please lead me
To break of day.

I have fallen, I'm frightened,
And my soul will weep.
Holy Shepherd, please find me,
Search for Your lost sheep.

In Your care I find comfort.
In Your love I sleep.
Come and seek me, my Shepherd,
Search for Your lost sheep.

From green pastures and still waters
I have gone astray.
Holy Spirit, please find me
And show me the way.

Holy Spirit, I thank You.
I've found my way.
Holy Shepherd, I thank You,
For break of day.

Though I've fallen, Your mercy
Helps me find the way
To green pastures and still waters;
On my knees, I've prayed.

Holy Spirit, I thank You.
You've shown me the way
As You offer forgiveness
And a brand-new day.

NAOMI TERRANELLA

THEREFORE, AS THE ELECT OF GOD, HOLY
AND BELOVED, PUT-ON TENDER MERCIES,
KINDNESS, HUMBLENESS OF MIND, MEEKNESS,
AND PATIENCE; BEARING WITH ONE ANOTHER,
AND FORGIVING ONE ANOTHER.

IF ANYONE HAS A COMPLAINT AGAINST
ANOTHER, EVEN AS CHRIST FORGAVE YOU, SO
YOU ALSO MUST DO.

BUT ABOVE ALL THESE THINGS PUT ON LOVE,
WHICH IS THE BOND OF PERFECTION. AND LET
THE PEACE OF GOD RULE IN YOUR HEARTS, TO
WHICH YOU WERE CALLED IN ONE BODY; AND
BE THANKFUL.

COLOSSIANS 3:12–15

BEHOLD, THE LAMB OF GOD!

JOHN 1:36

Mary Had a Little Lamb

Mary had a little lamb.
His name was Jesus Christ.
And everywhere that Jesus went
Good folks learned to be nice.
For Jesus taught that peace, hope, love;
These things add up to life.

NAOMI TERRANELLA

BLESSED BE THE LORD GOD, THE GOD OF
ISRAEL, WHO DOES WONDROUS THINGS! AND
BLESSED BE HIS GLORIOUS NAME FOREVER!

AND LET THE WHOLE EARTH BE FILLED WITH
HIS GLORY.

PSALM 72:18–19

My Best, Best Friend

Thank You, God, for this green earth,
The place of all of mankind's birth.

Where I am free to stay or roam
Or take a wife and make a home.

Where life is good and full of gain.
I thank You for the sun and rain.

You've made this earth a lovely place
And put such joy upon my face.

You've put it there for all to see,
That in my heart, my God loves me.

And thank You for family and friends
With lasting love that never ends;

And, mostly, You must surely see
I thank You, God, for making me.

RONALD TERRANELLA

OH COME, LET US SING TO THE LORD!
LET US SHOUT JOYFULLY TO THE ROCK OF
OUR SALVATION. LET US COME BEFORE HIS
PRESENCE WITH THANKSGIVING.

PSALM 95:1–2

My Gratitude

God, I'd like to sing to You my gratitude,
Forever, all the rest of my days.
I'd also like to thank You for loving me
And bring to You my very best praise.

When I feel weak, I fall on my knees;
Then, suddenly,
I hear the sound of children singing.
I feel a gentle breeze.
My burdens You ease.

When I'm afraid, I lift up my hands;
Then, lovingly,
I hear Your call.
You shelter my fall.
I fear not at all.

You hold me awhile
And lead me through the trial;
Then, once again,
You make me smile.

NAOMI TERRANELLA

JESUS CHRIST IS THE SAME YESTERDAY, TODAY AND FOREVER.

HEBREWS 13:8

My Soul Cries Out

My soul cries out
For the peace that I might know.
My soul cries out.
Help me let it go.

You are here with me
In my darkest hour of need,
And the pain will pass.
God's eternity will last.

Take me there,
Free of trouble, far from harms.
Take me there,
To the shelter of Your arms.

Suddenly, I hear You say,
"I'm aware of what you feel.
Don't forget My perfect plan:
For Heaven's very real."

Then I know, someday,
I'll be forever in Your care.
You are here with me,
With me always, everywhere.

NAOMI TERRANELLA

THEREFORE, IF ANYONE IS IN CHRIST, HE IS A
NEW CREATION; OLD THINGS HAVE PASSED
AWAY. BEHOLD, ALL THINGS HAVE BECOME
NEW.

2 CORINTHIANS 5:17

New

With You in my life,
There can be no regret;
And, forever,
My shoes won't wear.
And as I cross the Red Sea,
Not one toe will get wet.
I am safe for my Savior is there.

Though my frock may be old,
My soul is brand-new
For it is restored every day.
I walk with no fear
When I walk with You.
Thank you, Lord,
For showing the way.

New. New. Life brand-new.
New, Christ, in You.

For so many years, I wandered alone
'Till You led me to grace by Your hand.
I was down, lost, and cold,
Crying in emptiness;
Then You showed me the Promised Land.

Renewed by Your strength,
My steps are made firm.
Though I stumble, You shelter my fall.
I won't walk alone
Through this world's wilderness
If I'm led by my Savior's call.

New. New. Life brand-new.
New, abiding in You.

RONALD TERRANELLA

FOR I AM THE LORD, YOUR GOD, WHO TAKES
HOLD OF YOUR RIGHT HAND AND SAYS TO YOU,
DO NOT FEAR; I WILL HELP YOU.

ISAIAH 41:13

No Tragedy

No tragedy can frighten me.
I know, someday, I will be free.
A storm may last a little while,
But God's love conquers every trial.

He's waiting there for all of us
To jump into His Heaven's bus.

Why should I fear this earthly stuff
When I know God will be enough
To fill my soul with splendidness?
Just wait awhile. He'll fix this mess.

NAOMI TERRANELLA

Once Again

When I'm going in the wrong direction,
There You are with Your sin detection.

I stand accused, but wanting to be used
For Godly purpose once again.

As I pray to see Your vision,
I give thanks for Your conviction.

I feel my sin go into remission;
And now, I'm worthy of Your mission.

Once again, once again, once again.

NAOMI TERRANELLA

WHAT SHALL WE SAY THEN? SHALL WE
CONTINUE IN SIN THAT GRACE MAY ABOUND?

CERTAINLY NOT! HOW SHALL WE WHO DIED TO
SIN LIVE ANY LONGER IN IT?

ROMANS 6:1–2

Christ is born

Before Jesus was born, the world was extremely dark. Cruelty was common and accepted. The atrocities were horrible. Savage brutality was ruling this planet.

The words that Jesus spoke changed the world. His birth was predicted long before he was born. His birth was a miracle. He was born to enlighten the world about the joys of compassion. He spoke words of love, peace, kindness, mercy, and forgiveness.

The Bible's books of Matthew and Luke tell the story of Jesus' birth.

Today, that sweet, Jewish baby is often called "the light of the world."

SHE BROUGHT FORTH HER FIRSTBORN SON, AND WRAPPED HIM IN SWADDLING CLOTHES, AND LAID HIM IN A MANGER, BECAUSE THERE WAS NO ROOM FOR THEM IN THE INN.

AND THERE WERE IN THE SAME COUNTRY SHEPHERDS LIVING OUT IN THE FIELDS, KEEPING WATCH OVER THEIR FLOCK BY NIGHT.

AND, LO, AN ANGEL OF THE LORD STOOD BEFORE THEM, AND THE GLORY OF THE LORD SHONE AROUND THEM, AND THEY WERE GREATLY AFRAID. THEN THE ANGEL SAID TO THEM, "FEAR NOT; FOR, BEHOLD, I BRING YOU GOOD TIDINGS OF GREAT JOY WHICH WILL BE TO ALL PEOPLE. FOR THERE IS BORN TO YOU THIS DAY, IN THE CITY OF DAVID, A SAVIOR, WHO IS CHRIST THE LORD. AND THIS SHALL BE A SIGN TO YOU: YOU WILL FIND A BABE WRAPPED IN SWADDLING CLOTHES, LYING IN A MANGER."

AND SUDDENLY THERE WAS WITH THE ANGEL A MULTITUDE OF HEAVENLY HOST PRAISING GOD, AND SAYING, "GLORY TO GOD IN THE HIGHEST, AND PEACE ON EARTH, GOOD WILL TOWARD MEN."

LUKE 2:7–14

One Great Star

(a Hanukkah and Christmas Poem)

When I was a child, my mother taught me
The Bible has two testaments we need to read.
The old gives golden rules to heed,
The new, redeeming grace.

She said, "Make new friends, but keep the old.
One is silver and the other is gold."

Jesus, Rabbi of the Jews,
Had heritage we must not refuse,

Favor from our God on high,
This is the reason why
Jews traveled afar
To One Great Star.

These are the gifts we all can share
During God's time of year:

Hanukkah lights would tell the tale;
Oil would still be there.
Nothing that God would not provide;
Nothing there left to fear.

Babe in a manger giving light;
Giving our souls a new delight.
Making it all so clear, that night,
Shining a beam of hope, so bright.

Traveling far to One Great Star.

These are the gifts we all can share
During God's time of year.

NAOMI TERRANELLA

Precious

The most precious thing
That a person can own
Is not gold, or diamonds,
Or a royalty throne.
The most precious thing
Is to have You call us Your own.

RONALD TERRANELLA

A NEW COMMANDMENT I GIVE TO YOU, THAT
YOU LOVE ONE ANOTHER; AS I HAVE LOVED
YOU, THAT YOU ALSO LOVE ONE ANOTHER.

JOHN 13:34

Purple People

If all people were purple,
How happy life could be!

Skin color wouldn't matter.
Wouldn't that be lovely!

We'd all love one another
As God wants us to be.

There'd be no reason for fighting,
For feuds, or for crime.

And we'd rejoice in God's presence;
But now, we must give Him time

To solve the hate riddle
And make this world rhyme.

NAOMI TERRANELLA

Remember Mom
(To my daughter, Tracy, my Joy)

Remember you and me going to the zoo.
Remember you and me sitting in a tree.
Remember you and me when my time is through
For I will always, always be with you.

Remember you and me and our poetry.
Remember you and me smiling through the tears.
Remember you and me through the coming years
For I will always hold you through your fears.

Remember you and me growing up to be
A tiny, solid, loving family.

Now, take a moment.
Feel God's love for you.
Let Him take you back through your life's review.

Remember walking on the moonlit beach.
Remember words of "Kumbayah" you knew.
Remember teachers you would like to teach.
Remember stacks of cool library books due.
Remember Horton, your pink monkey,
Playing songs and peek-a-boo.

Now, let your faith in Spiritual Power
Come to light and be as new.
For through God's power, you will see the signs
That I will, always, send to you:
A singing bird, a gentle breeze,
A celebration rainbow,

And you will know.

Remember, always, my dear daughter,
That your mother loves you so.

NAOMI TERRANELLA

DO NOT BE ANXIOUS ABOUT ANYTHING, BUT
IN EVERYTHING, BY PRAYER AND PETITION,
WITH THANKSGIVING, PRESENT YOUR
REQUESTS TO GOD, AND THE PEACE OF GOD,
WHICH TRANSCENDS ALL UNDERSTANDING,
WILL GUARD YOUR HEARTS AND MINDS IN
JESUS CHRIST.

PHILIPPIANS 4:6–7

Resurrect My Soul

Let Your love roll this rock; roll it away.
Let Your love fill my heart; mold it like clay.
Help me, Father, I pray.

My hope in You has slipped into a cave.
I need you like the ocean needs the wave.
Come and make me whole. Resurrect my soul.

I know you can release me from this pain.
Restore me, Holy Spirit, shine again.
Come and make me whole. Resurrect my soul.

Help me, Father, for I long to know Your plan.
Lift me, hold me, guide me to Your promised land.
Come and make me whole. Resurrect my soul.

You hear my prayers. You know I'm lost.
You warm my heart and melt the frost.
You come and make me whole again.
Your perfect peace comes rushing in.
You, Holy Spirit, Faithful Friend,
Have saved me once again.

NAOMI TERRANELLA

Satan's Regret

I almost had you, didn't I?
Captured in my thorny thicket.
I helped you tell a little lie
And saved you from that speeding ticket.

Walking from that grocery store,
You noticed you had too much change.
Oh well, it's just a little more,
And you deserve it anyway.

You're just a sinner, after all,
Practicing your given nature.
Set by Adam in the garden.
Simple nomenclature.

Then a voice, from far away,
Came resonating through the wood
To interrupt my evil play
And lead you toward the good.

He sent His Son to die for you,
In agony, for mercy's sake.
His body hung upon the cross
Forgiving your mistakes.

You turned your face away from me,
Admitting that your life's a mess,
And reached out to your Father
Striving for a life of righteousness.

Still, I'll be ever present, Dear,
To offer you the moon and sky.
Though you resist me, year by year,
I almost had you, didn't I?

DONALD TERRANELLA

Satanic Amnesia

Never forget what Satan has taken.
He started our trouble, leading man to his fall.
He tricked us to turn our focus from Jesus
And made us feel unworthy of our Savior's call.

He is the deceiver. His words are all lies.
He hates us much more than anyone can.
He, diligently, works to loosen all ties
And destroy communication between God and man.

He, somehow, evokes satanic amnesia
And makes us forget the pain that he causes.
How else can he tempt us to repeat behavior
That leads to destruction and amasses losses?

His fury's upon us. He hates with a passion.
He will rob, steal, and kill whenever he can.
He has taken from Heaven one third of the angels
And is raising his tally of men.

We must always beware of how we've been tempted
And resist that enticement when it's thrown in our face
Or be subject to suffer the same consequences
That led us to ruin in the first place.

Do not give the devil one ounce of attention
For, in return, he will give back a ton of pain.
What value to you is a moment of pleasure
If frustration and torment, in the end, is your gain?

You can trust Satan to be mistrusted,
So be on your guard when he nears,
Or he'll win you his gift of damnation
And eternity's not measured in years.

RONALD TERRANELLA

GET BEHIND ME, SATAN! YOU ARE AN OFFENSE TO ME, FOR YOU ARE NOT MINDFUL OF THE THINGS OF GOD, BUT THE THINGS OF MEN.

MATTHEW 16:23

Senses

Thank you for my senses, Lord,
To smell the very air I breathe,
To hear a child's laughter,
To see an autumn leaf,

To taste the nectar of Your fruit,
To touch another person's hand
Lets me know, beyond refute,
It's all by Your command.

Of all the senses You've bestowed,
Upon this fleeting drop of dew,
Is sure the sense You've given me
To store my faith in You.

DONALD TERRANELLA

Shy-la

Just sitting, relaxing, a lump on a log.
The last thing on earth that I need is a dog.

The feeding, the walking, the cleaning-up hair.
Picking-up droppings is a horrid affair.

All running, and playing, and lessons to teach.
Sometimes at night we walk on the beach.

Shy-la's her name, my perpetual shadow.
She flickers and flits like a lamb in a meadow.

Somedays, aside, by a quaint fishing hole;
Or I'll take her around for a sociable stroll.

A good-looking K-9, or so I've been told,
And she's such a good listener—someone to hold.

This stage in my life, like the lifting of fog,
So glad I decided to get me a dog.

DONALD TERRANELLA

So, You Don't Believe in God?

Why won't you
    Open your eyes, look to the skies,
    See what is real, love that we feel,
    This comes from God.

Or can you
    Make me a rose? Everyone knows
    This can be done only by One.
    This comes from God.

When will you
    Laugh in the snow, see the rainbow,
    Feel the sunshine, know that you're fine,
    Love what you see, dare to be free.

His gifts to you. These come from God.

NAOMI TERRANELLA

Someday

Scientists say
Rainbows come from gasses.
Psychologists say
Psychosis comes from masses.

Don't need your scientific explanation.
I live with joy and expectation

To live in love above the clouds,
To leave the pitfalls of the crowds,
To be with Jesus
Someday.

NAOMI TERRANELLA

THE LORD IS MY SHEPHERD; I SHALL NOT
WANT. HE MAKES ME TO LIE DOWN IN GREEN
PASTURES; HE LEADS ME BESIDE THE STILL
WATERS. HE RESTORES MY SOUL; HE LEADS
ME IN THE PATHS OF RIGHTEOUSNESS FOR HIS
NAME'S SAKE.

YEA, THOUGH I WALK THROUGH THE VALLEY
OF THE SHADOW OF DEATH, I WILL FEAR NO
EVIL; FOR YOU ARE WITH ME; YOUR ROD AND
YOUR STAFF, THEY COMFORT ME. YOU PREPARE
A TABLE BEFORE ME IN THE PRESENCE OF MY
ENEMIES; YOU ANOINT MY HEAD WITH OIL;
MY CUP RUNS OVER. SURELY GOODNESS AND
MERCY SHALL FOLLOW ME ALL THE DAYS OF MY
LIFE, AND I WILL DWELL IN THE HOUSE OF THE
LORD FOREVER.

PSALM 23

Still, Still Water

Lead me by the still, still water.
Plant me in a field so green.
We'll have fun.
Thy will be done.

You are the One
Who calms the sea.
Lead me by the still, still water.
Come and rescue me.

Some things will never change.
Past, present, future,
You'll remain.
You're still the One
Who formed us all.
Help me to listen
To Your call.

Still, still water calms my soul.
Fields so green soften life's toll.

NAOMI TERRANELLA

Stones

What if the stones of the earth could speak?
Imagine the stories they would tell.
From the ones a foot be dashed upon
To those built in a wishing well.

Were five of them once honored
That David chose them for his sling
To end Goliath's tyranny
Against his God and king?

Can stones feel shame to be picked-up
To execute Miss Magdalene?
I wonder if they felt relief
When dropped back to the green?

What of the ones were rolled aside,
Releasing Lazarus, and then our Lord?
Already they speak volumes
Without uttering a word.

Golgotha was in the shape of a skull,
Where God was deftly crucified.
How could this stone describe the way
His prosecutors lied?

DONALD TERRANELLA

Subtraction by Addiction

I once thought you legend, now see that you're real,
Collecting our souls like a fisherman's creel.
You promise a happy euphorious place.
I've traveled your lies and see your true face.

Carnivorous creature, thou bearest distain.
As you hollow our hearts and gnaw at our brains.
Ominous entity, hideous beast,
Our thoughts are your shelter, our dreams are your feast.

Thank God that this being possesses a will
Which bares you full-naked and feeds you with swill.
If you had your way, by your own accord,
You'd drop souls from your hand into the fiord.

You'd drop them deep, to hide them well,
And leave them with an empty shell.
But precious souls, that you would have poured,
Are not yours to touch. They belong to the Lord.

You'll be with me always, cold breath on my back,
To reenter my world as a snake through a crack.
I wonder, in Eden, if you were "the one."
If not, 'twas your mentor, oh dangerous son.

In search of an answer, as daily I pray,
I wish you could be slain some conventional way.
But one cannot harm one who will never feel.
To strike you would shatter Excalibur's steel.

If our paths should cross on the street someday,
I'll pretend not to know you and send you away.
Yes, I'll bid you to ride your odiferous steed.
Of course, you won't miss me. You've others to bleed.

So, you might as well halt your malignant attack
For the power of God can give us back.

DONALD TERRANELLA

Super Soul Treat

The other day when
I started to pray,
For God to put me
Where He wants me to be,
I heard His still voice tell me,
"Get in the mood.
Go out and find yourself
A little super soul food."

So, He put me in a place
Called the Homeless Outreach.
It's a cool, little place
Down in Oceanside Beach,
Where those who need a home
Can get a bite to eat,
And those who lend a hand
Can get a super soul treat.

I marveled at the sky so blue.
I kissed the ocean breeze.
I watched the homeless come to life
As we all prayed on our knees.
Then, Brother Dan, the preacher man,
Helped us laugh and sing awhile.
I felt my heart feel joy in life
As I felt our Father's smile.

Super soul treat,
So super sweet.
So glad our Father gave to me
A super soul treat.

NAOMI TERRANELLA

In the book of Mark, Jesus used the word "physician" in a parable. Jesus was not a medical doctor. He came to offer the world much more than medical advice. Jesus came to offer hope to the sick and to lighten our burden of sin.

NOW IT HAPPENED, AS JESUS WAS DINING IN LEVI'S HOUSE, THAT MANY TAX COLLECTORS AND SINNERS ALSO SAT TOGETHER WITH JESUS AND HIS DISCIPLES; FOR THERE WERE MANY, AND THEY FOLLOWED HIM.

AND WHEN THE SCRIBES AND PHARISEES SAW HIM EATING WITH THE TAX COLLECTORS AND SINNERS, THEY SAID TO HIS DISCIPLES, "HOW IS IT THAT HE EATS AND DRINKS WITH TAX COLLECTORS AND SINNERS?"

WHEN JESUS HEARD IT, HE SAID TO THEM, "THOSE WHO ARE WELL HAVE NO NEED OF A PHYSICIAN, BUT THOSE WHO ARE SICK. I DID NOT COME TO CALL THE RIGHTEOUS, BUT SINNERS, TO REPENTANCE."

MARK 2:15–17

Take This Job and Love It

I have a Boss who's good to me,
Not like the one I had.
This One, He looks out for me,
But the other one was bad.

My old boss wouldn't pay me,
But my new One paid my debt.
My old boss, he took everything,
But now my needs are met.

I used to put in overtime
Just slaving day and night,
But now my job is easy
And all my burdens light.

Sometimes, I still work overtime,
But oh, the pay is great!
The joy it brings encourages me
To never show up late.

The benefits of working here
Are more than words can say.
The inheritance of Heaven
And undying love is the pay.

The health plan is the greatest
For it can cure all things.
The Physician knows the latest
Of the healing God's love brings.

And, as for my retirement,
The plan is really great:
A mansion and new body.
Man, I can hardly wait!

Part of my job description
Is to bear long-lasting fruit.
I praise my Boss, for all He's done,
On lyre, drum, and flute.

I stand by my coworkers
And hire all I can.
And humbly thank my loving Lord,
Who saved this wretched man.

I quit the boss I used to have,
Who didn't pay me well.
In fact, he cost me everything
As far as I could tell.

My new Boss gave His all for me
From His abundant wealth.
He's worked Himself to death,
You see, to save me, gave Himself.

RONALD TERRANELLA

**TEACH ME YOUR WAY, O LORD, AND LEAD ME IN
A SMOOTH PATH.**

PSALM 27:11

Teach Me to Learn

We must accept the chastening
That we receive in life
As sin removing surgery,
God's discipline, the knife.

The Master forges iron
And iron sharpens such;
Through hammering and fire,
The Lord availeth much.
As the athlete finds his mark
Then runs the race to win it,
So does the sculptor cut the stone
To find the treasure in it.

Our Lord equips His soldiers
To triumph in His task,
Not sent into the battle
Without supplies or flask.
Like pruning to a flower
Or weeding to a lawn,
God gives renewing power
From trusting in His Son.

The Carpenter will shape the wood
Then smooth it as He pleases.
Before He did, it was no good.
I thank you, Savior Jesus.

RONALD TERRANELLA

Thanks for the Key

I thank You for the blessings
You give me every day:
Forgiveness for confessing
And answers when I pray;

The smiles on children's faces;
The gifts upon my plate;
My heart filled from Your graces;
With love, where once was hate;

A chance to be a man again;
I have no fear of death.
Not empty like a mannequin,
Blessed beyond my last breath.

Inside my heart, You're with me.
Your welcome presence known.
When I am down, You lift me.
I never stand alone.

In my place, You died for me.
Forever, I am Yours.
And, since You've risen, shared the key
To open Heaven's door.

RONALD TERRANELLA

**AND I WILL GIVE YOU THE KEYS OF THE
KINGDOM OF HEAVEN, AND WHATEVER YOU
BIND ON EARTH WILL BE BOUND IN HEAVEN.**

MATTHEW 16:19

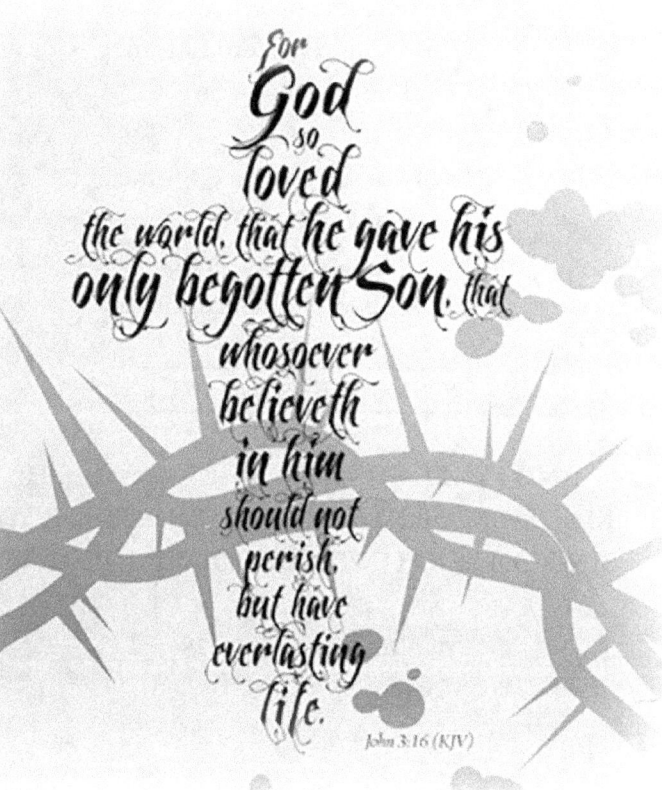

For God so loved the world, that he gave his only begotten Son, that whosoever believeth in him should not perish, but have everlasting life.

John 3:16 (KJV)

The Cross

They hung our Lord upon a cross,
A deed that lives in infamy.
Now, we hang one 'round our necks,
Forgetting not His agony.

A symbol known throughout the world,
Whatever land we live in.
A sign that shows such mercy
That the nailer was forgiven.

DONALD TERRANELLA

**...GO AND BEAR FRUIT... THESE THINGS
I COMMAND YOU, THAT YOU LOVE ONE
ANOTHER.**

JOHN 15:16–17

The Fruit of God's Vine

God's love is like a seed planted inside
A soul that is no longer willing to hide
In the soil within, reaching out of the sin
To a glorious light, Heaven's blossoms in sight.

Lord, plant Your seed in this heart of mine.
May the soul of this longing heart
Bear the fruit of God's vine.

For the fruit of the Spirit is love, joy, and peace;
Patience and kindness; goodness and faith;
Gentleness and self-control;[11]
Grace and mercy entwined.
May the soul of this longing heart
Bear the fruit of God's vine.

Lord, plant Your seed in Your perfect time.
May the soul of this longing heart
Bear the fruit of God's vine.

NAOMI TERRANELLA

[11] Galatians 5:22–23

The Judge, The Great I Am

My injured soul
You alone can judge.
My heart, when broken,
Feels Your gentle nudge.

You told me I'm Your sheltered lamb
And that I'm welcome; but I ran,
From You, who judged my innocence
And found me guilty of not having sense.

But You still love me as I am,
Within Your hand, at Your command.
No longer must I hide my face.
You've given me Your healing grace.

I've learned to love the Son of Man.
I thank the Great I Am.

NAOMI TERRANELLA

The Lord's Prayer

OUR FATHER, IN HEAVEN, HALLOWED BE YOUR NAME. YOUR KINGDOM COME. YOUR WILL BE DONE ON EARTH AS IT IS IN HEAVEN.

GIVE US THIS DAY OUR DAILY BREAD, AND FORGIVE US OUR DEBTS, AS WE FORGIVE OUR DEBTORS.

AND DO NOT LEAD US INTO TEMPTATION BUT DELIVER US FROM THE EVIL ONE.

FOR YOURS IS THE KINGDOM AND THE POWER AND THE GLORY, FOREVER AND EVER.

AMEN

MATTHEW 6:9–13

ONE THING I HAVE DESIRED OF THE LORD,
THAT I WILL SEEK: THAT I MAY DWELL IN THE
HOUSE OF THE LORD, ALL THE DAYS OF MY
LIFE, TO BEHOLD THE BEAUTY OF THE LORD,
AND TO INQUIRE IN HIS TEMPLE.

PSALM 27:4

The Master Builder

I live in a house remodeled by God
Complete with all the trimmings.
But before He came and fixed it up,
Wretched were its beginnings.

First, He had to gut the dump,
And there it stood so humble.
Then, He swept the whole place clean,
So that I wouldn't stumble.

He then hauled the junk away
That cluttered-up my yard.
I thought it looked impossible,
But for Him it wasn't hard.

He began with my foundation
And set up piers of rock.
Then framed the wall with timbers
Made from the finest stock.

He set the beams where they should be,
Instead of where they were,
Adjusting everything just right
Like a good carpenter.

I tried to help Him when I could,
But just kept bending nails.
He said, "Don't worry, I'll get that."
And His swing never fails.

He built some stairs that led to Him
Against a sturdy wall.
And then attached a railing,
So that I wouldn't fall.

Next, He did the plumbing
To bring fresh water in.
He then installed some lines for power
Where only holes had been.

He hung the drywall beautifully,
Then smoothed out all rough edges.
And while the plaster hardened,
He dug some holes for hedges.

He always worked long hours.
It seemed like day and night.
He toiled when I went to sleep
And was there before daylight.

He painted, patched, and carpeted
And made old things brand-new.
His labors brought me peace and joy,
But still He wasn't through.

He filled up all my cupboards
With everything I needed
And planted His protecting hedge,
Then raked the leaves and weeded.

He took the junk that I still wanted
And said I didn't need it.
And, trusting Him, I gave it up.
His purpose was not defeated.

Now came the time that I dreaded:
The time to pay the bill.
But He said, "It's been paid in full
By my Son's work on Skull Hill."

Then, He climbed into His truck
And parked it right out front.
He said, "You can just call on Me
If there's any lack or want."

So now, I see Him every day
For He's become my friend.
I know that He will stay with me
On Him I can depend.

RONALD TERRANELLA

The Mirror of Reality

I see my every error
When I look into the mirror.
Seeking Your grace,
I long to see Your face
Shining clearly through my eyes,
But my sin I can't disguise.

I confess my mistake.
Then, my soul You quickly take
Back into Your arms
To shelter me from harms
That I've done to myself
When I put you on a shelf.

But, You waited for me
To accept eternity:
To see You loving me
In the mirror of reality.

NAOMI TERRANELLA

The Nursing Home

No fear. Help me reach out for another.
No fear. Help me extend them a hand.
No fear. Lord, let us love one another
As we walk in the light of Your plan.

There he sits in his first nursing home
Feeling all alone.
I hear his son discussing his father.
I hear him say:

"Dad cannot read; he cannot walk;
He cannot work. What can he do?"

Can't we read the Bible our Father wrote?
Can't we walk in the light of His plan?
Can't we work to live as our Savior taught?

What can your dad do?
He'll bring out the Jesus in you.

No fear.

There she sits in her last nursing home
Feeling all alone.
I see the doctor discussing her fate.
I hear him say:

"She will not see; she will not hear;
She will not speak. What will she be?"

Can't you see how much I need her now?
Can't you hear God's voice calling me?

Can't I say how thankful I am for her?
For she is a precious gift to me.

What will she be?
She'll be compassion in me.

No Fear.

NAOMI TERRANELLA

THE BLIND RECEIVE THEIR SIGHT, AND THE
LAME WALK, THE LEPERS ARE CLEANSED, AND
THE DEAF HEAR, THE DEAD ARE RAISED UP, AND
THE POOR HAVE THE GOSPEL PREACHED TO
THEM.

MATTHEW 11:5–5

The Road I'd Crossed

I once walked down the Worldly Path
That led me to despair.
Oh sure, it ran past Pleasure Street;
So, I spent a season there.

Then I cruised down to Plenty Way
Where money was the key.
But soon I wondered, did I own
Or did my wealth own me?

I made a left on Drunkard Court
To see what I'd been missin'.
And there I gave up everything
And woke one day in prison.

But drinking doesn't get you life
(Well not all at one time.)
And when I left the county jail,
I began my life of crime.

I spent some time at Hurt You Road,
The street before Hurt Me.
And got a job from Satan
But worked all day for free.

I circled down Dope Ave.,
Man, what a hairy scene!
Then, somehow, changed my point of view
And tried to become clean.

For there I sat at Sin and Death;
This corner made me scared.
I looked to find a friendly face
But found nobody cared.

Yet still, I went on searching
And realized I was lost.
I stumbled in the darkness
To find the road I'd crossed.

I cried, "Oh Lord, please help me!"
And soon there was this Man.
I thought I'd seen His face before;
So, I turned around and ran.

He called out, "Do not be afraid
For I mean you no harm."
I stopped and He said,
"Follow Me, and I will lead you home."

I knew that I could trust this Man,
Who seemed to be here waiting.
So, when He reached, I took His hand
With little hesitating.

He walked me down to Charity Way;
And there, we dined together.
And then, He gave His coat to me
To guard me from foul weather.

Next, we strolled down to Peace Lane
And rested by still waters.
There, I met His family,
His Father's sons and daughters.

It didn't take me anytime
To love my newfound friends.
I'd wished to have a family
Before my time here ends.

I noticed that the clouds were gone,
And the sun was shining bright.
And I no longer was afraid
For dark gave way to light.

We walked away; I waved good-bye;
They said, "We'll see you later."
My Partner said, "These things you seek
You'll find—and so much greater."

We turned the bend, and I stopped cold
For we were in Pain Alley.
But He lifted me and kept me safe
Until we reached Hope Valley.

It was there I gave my life to Him
And vowed to be His slave.
In return, He'd be my Savior
Through life and beyond the grave.

I always will be grateful
For all that He has done
And thankful for that faithful day
That God sent me His Son.

RONALD TERRANELLA

THOSE WHO WAIT ON THE LORD SHALL RENEW
THEIR STRENGTH; THEY SHALL RUN AND NOT
BE WEARY, THEY SHALL WALK AND NOT FAINT.

ISAIAH 40:31

The Tears of God

He loves us one and all--even the worst.
When we are in need, He quenches our thirst.

When our souls are barren, He provides abundance
And forgives our sins in constant redundance.

Our thoughts are disgusting; our actions are worse;
Our stealing and lusting; the greed we put first.

Our lies are so common; our hatred accepted;
And still, through His love, we are not rejected.

His gifts are most special. We act like He owes us
And rarely appreciate the wonders He shows us.

The most precious thing that a person can own
Is not gold or riches or an emperor's throne.

From God, this we've taken; yet He hates us not.
Yes, even forgives us, this treacherous lot.

He's torn down the curtain and darkened the sky
For could even God watch His only Son die?

The tears of God.

RONALD TERRANELLA

The Words in Red
(Books of Matthew, Mark, Luke, and John)

I'm flipping through the Bible,
While in this church I sit,
And I'm trying hard to keep-up;
But I'm having such a fit

For I'm trying to figure-out what was said.
I focus as my eyes fall on the words in red.
The thoughts are simple, there, to me;
I learn that His blood sets me free.

Feeling bad 'cause I've lost my place.
Feeling shame upon my face
For I haven't learned this verse or that.
I try to keep my ignorance under my hat.

Then, suddenly, it's clear to me;
I know that His blood sets me free.
Jesus died for you and me.
His promise is eternity.

NAOMI TERRANELLA

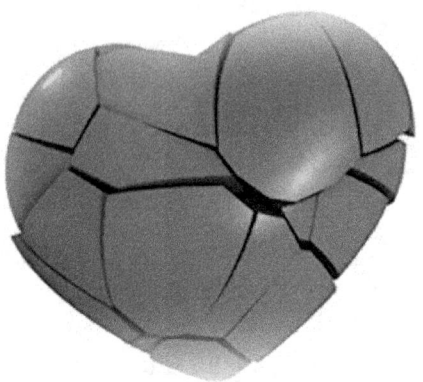

This Broken Heart

Where exactly am I, Lord,
Or does it really, even matter?
For You've walked so many thousand miles,
Before You reached for Heaven's ladder.

The ones I cared for brought me anguish,
Deception as a form of art.
Until my love of them was vanquished.
Thank You for this broken heart.

The life I led, awhile back,
Was cold and dark and damp and grey.
Until You gave me strength
I lacked And brightly lit my way.

I see You've placed me purposely;
Like dewdrops on each blade of grass;
Like stars above that light the night
And everyone I pass.

How can Your hand be so precise,
When Heaven seems so far away,
To nudge us toward the path of life?
(We tend to go astray.)

If it weren't for disappointment,
From old lives, we might never part
To seek Your spirit for anointment.
Thank You for this broken heart.

DONALD TERRANELLA

HE HEALS THE BROKEN-HEARTED AND BINDS UP THEIR WOUNDS.

PSALM 147:3

This Shattered Vessel

I need for You to mend me, God,
For broken is my heart.
I don't know if it came that way
Or when it fell apart.

It has a couple holes in it
And really needs a cleaning.
I know that it's not working well
For my life lacks all meaning.

I can't find all the pieces,
And I don't have any glue.
I've heard that You can fix me, Lord;
So, I give myself to You.

He took this shattered vessel
And threw the junk away,
Then formed for me a brand-new heart,
As the potter does with clay.

He smoothed out the rough edges
And gently shaped it with His hands,
Then washed away the cuts and scars,
As the ocean does the sands.

Next, He added brilliant colors
And gave new life to what was plain,
Then washed away the defects
And rinsed them down the drain.

When I reached out to help Him,
I nearly knocked it to the floor.
He said to me, "Just wait out front,
But please don't shut the door."

He watched it cure so patiently,
Then coated it with glaze;
And then it shined so clearly,
Obscured no longer by the haze.

Now came the time to fire it
To make it strong and hard.
He sealed it with His spirit,
So that it wouldn't be marred.

He pulled it from the oven
And showed great skill quite unsurpassed.
This new thing was a work of art
And really built to last.

Now came the time that worried me:
The price for what the Master made.
But He said, "It's a gift for free.
My Son's already paid."

The heart that He returned to me
Was nothing like the old.
It came with two life guarantees
And a pass to where the streets are gold.

The maintenance plan was perfect
For He was there each time I called.
I read His care instructions;
And when attacked, I was not mauled.

I thank my God for all He does
And even more for what He's done:
Restoring what I could not fix
By sending me His Son.

RONALD TERRANELLA

To Satan

You take my heart and twist it
'Till my thoughts are gray and ashen;
And then, you try to strip me
Of my soul and my compassion.

I must say, "No! This will not do
For I know right from wrong.
So, just be gone. Get out of here!
You will not take my song."

NAOMI TERRANELLA

AWAY WITH YOU, SATAN! FOR IT IS WRITTEN,
"YOU SHALL WORSHIP THE LORD YOUR GOD,
AND HIM ONLY YOU SHALL SERVE."

MATTHEW 4:10

Use Me, Lord

Heavenly Father,
Give me the will
To follow Your cross,
Shining peace on a hill.

I know I fall short
Of Your model to follow.
Put You in my heart.
Don't let me be hollow.

Use me Lord, please use me.

Heavenly Father,
Show me the way
To lighten my heart
Through Your walk day by day.

You fill-in the void
Of a heart that is aching.
I offer my will.
It's Yours for the taking.

Use me, Lord, please use me.

NAOMI TERRANELLA

**YOUR WORD IS A LAMP UNTO MY FEET AND A
LIGHT UNTO MY PATH.**

PSALM 119:105

Vagabond

Don't know which way I'm going
Or which road I'm on.
I'm feeling like
An emotional vagabond.

But there's one thing that I'm sure of,
Wherever I might land:
I'm sitting, securely,
In the palm of Your hand.

I thank the Great I Am.

NAOMI TERRANELLA

We Are Recovering
(WAR on drugs)

We're standing on the battlefield
The casualties are high.
If we don't stand together,
We will surely die.

We must have a battle plan,
And follow it to the tee,
To fend off the intentions
Of this cunning enemy.

His methods are quite powerful.
He topples strong and valiant men,
Strewn as by a tidal wave,
Dashed time and time again.

Also, he is baffling,
Exploiting every word,
Infiltrating every nook
Of weakness he has heard.

He runs right up among us
And leads us to a dangerous place;
And though we've been deceived before,
He lies right to our face.

And so, we need a sentry
To ring the bell when trouble's near,
One who will never fall asleep
Or run away in fear,

To jump down from the parapet
And join the fight with sword in hand.
But He can only keep those safe
Who follow His command.

Potential doom awaits us.
So, we call to God in prayer.
For this killer is all over us
And isn't fighting fair.

We need to fight with tooth and nail,
To keep this murderer at bay,
And scramble safe to higher ground.
It's just twelve steps away.

Alone, we cannot beat this foe
With just our single spears and dirks.
But with our God, we'll put him down
For He can do great works.

RONALD TERRANELLA

**I HAVE HEARD YOUR PRAYERS; I HAVE SEEN
YOUR TEARS. SURELY, I WILL HEAL YOU.**

2 KINGS 20:5

IF WE LIVE IN THE SPIRIT, LET US ALSO WALK IN THE SPIRIT.

GALATIANS 5:25

What Would I Give?

What would I give to walk this earth like You?
What would I say if every word were true?
What would it cost? What suffering? What strife?
What's the reward?
The truth: eternal life.

How can I love You a little more than me?
How can I show You things no one wants to see?
How can You love me in times of pain and loss?
How about a memory:
The dawn came through a cross.

NAOMI TERRANELLA

Whenever We Fail

Whenever we fail
To walk in God's light,
There are times
When we might
Think He'll desert us,
Take back His love,
Never to lead us
To Heaven above.

During these times
As we search for His light,
His Bible can guide us
To make our lives bright.

For God truly loves us.
From Him, we can't depart.
He looks inside;
He sees our hearts
And gives us brand-new starts.

NAOMI TERRANELLA

Who Knows Jesus?

You'd think all would know Jesus
But not so many do.
I thank the Lord for knowing me.
Be sure He knows you too.

The very stars know Jesus.
They heralded His birth.
They shone upon a manger
When God came down to earth.

The wind and seas know Jesus,
Obeying His command.
The angry ocean humbly bowed
When God lifted His hand.

Those who know Him all delight
In Him next to God's seat.
The angels all know Jesus
And worship at His feet.

All of the demons know Him
And tremble at His sight.
His very name from earnest lips
Will make them flee from fright.

The children know who Jesus is.
They just might know Him best;
For they're not yet polluted
By perversions but are blessed.

The fish all know who Jesus is.
For Him, they'll brave the net.
They'll swallow whole a prophet
Or see God's tax is met.

The stones all know who Jesus is.
He guides them from the sling.
If people would not shout for joy,
The very rocks would sing.

The waters know who Jesus is.
For Him, they'll become wine
And quench the thirst of those who drink,
Forever, for all time.

The darkness knows who Jesus is,
But that's what most prefer;
For when the light of God is near,
It shows what fools we were.

Blindness knows who Jesus is,
And so does leprosy.
They both flee from believing souls
Whom Jesus has set free.

Death knows Jesus very well
And is subject to the King of Kings,
Who took the keys and shut up Hell.
Oh Death, where is your sting?[12]

Who knows who knows who Jesus is?
Only the Lord can tell.
God only knows who knows His Son.
The rest will know of Hell.

RONALD TERRANELLA

THE SPIRIT OF THE LORD IS UPON ME, BECAUSE
THE LORD HAS ANOINTED ME TO PREACH GOOD
TIDINGS TO THE LOWLY. HE HAS SENT ME TO
HEAL THE BROKENHEARTED, TO PROCLAIM
LIBERTY TO CAPTIVES, AND THE OPENING OF THE
PRISON TO THOSE WHO ARE BOUND.

ISAIAH 61:1

Without Walls

I once was a captive of envy,
A chain-bearing prisoner of strife.
I was shackled by greed,
In a stockade of hate,
And was facing damnation for life.

My jailer I saw in the mirror,
In my cell where I stood all alone.
For the keys to freedom,
I, myself, threw away
By forsaking my Savior's throne.

I was caught, for my crimes, red-handed.
My prints were all over the scene.
My actions recorded on camera.
There was no chance to get away clean.

So, I confessed and asked for mercy.
But, in my heart, I knew I was through.
To my surprise, He said, "Son, I forgive you,
And I'll tell you what I'm going to do."

Then, He took from me all of my shackles
And tore up my charges on the shelf.
Then, you wouldn't believe what that loving Man did.
He put my cuffs on Himself!

He said, "You are free to go now."
And He let the guard lead Him away.
But before He walked out of the throne room,
He said, "Take my peace on your way."

He gave to me all of His riches
And cleansed me of all of my filth.
Then, He left me completely pardoned
By serving my sentence Himself.

As I passed through those doors into freedom
And entered into heaven's halls,
God's light shined from all directions
In the place I now stand without walls.

RONALD TERRANELLA

Write On

A pencil or pen or crayons conceal
An idea or drawing or poem revealed;
A word to enlighten a heart that is down;
Or music without ever making a sound;

The scribbles of children that parents call art;
A master's first scrolling, revealed from the heart;
A businessman's tally; a schoolboy's first letter;
A name in an alley; or something much better;

A verse from the Bible, encouraging love;
The gift of a drawing, inspired from above;
A card from a child, trying her best.
The tools are essential. The heart does the rest.

RONALD TERRANELLA

DIRECT MY STEPS BY YOUR WORD, AND LET NO INIQUITY HAVE DOMINION OVER ME

PSALM 119:133

Your Faithful Fan

Lord, I am Your faithful fan
Longing to follow You wherever I can.
Lead me to Your promised land.
I'm Your faithful fan.

Help me see this world's Your stage;
Hear Your melodies, age-to-age;
Sing Your praises as You write the page.
I'm Your faithful fan.

Lord, I pray, 'till my life is through,
You'll find merit in things I do
As I offer my praise to You.
I'm Your faithful fan.

NAOMI TERRANELLA

**GIVE THANKS TO THE LORD, FOR HE IS GOOD!
HIS FAITHFUL LOVE ENDURES FOREVER.**

1 CHRONICLES 16:34

BLESSED BE THE NAME OF THE LORD FROM THIS TIME FORTH AND FOREVERMORE! FROM THE RISING OF THE SUN TO ITS GOING DOWN, THE LORD'S NAME IS TO BE PRAISED.

PSALM 113:2–3

Your Sunset

As You close Your day
In Your gentle way,
I renew my trust in You.

May Your will be mine
As You take Your time
Telling me exactly what to do:

Trust in You.
Never doubt Your plan for me.
Trust in You
For I'm where I ought to be:
In Your hand, in Your care,
Knowing You are always there
Holding me.

Holding me with blessings
And peace, beyond compare.
Colors so caressing
As Your twilight fills the air.

Now, the sky's aglow
With Your sunset show.
Beauty takes my breath away.
Heaven's shining light
Fades from day to night,
And You tell me as I pray:

Trust in You.
Never doubt Your plan for me.
Trust in You
For I'm where I ought to be:
In Your hand, in Your care,
Knowing You are always there
Holding me.

NAOMI TERRANELLA

Jesus Said

"LET NOT YOUR HEART BE TROUBLED, YOU
BELIEVE IN GOD, BELIEVE ALSO IN ME."

"IN MY FATHER'S HOUSE ARE MANY MANSIONS.
I GO TO PREPARE A PLACE FOR YOU."

"AND IF I GO AND PREPARE A PLACE FOR YOU,
I WILL COME AGAIN AND RECEIVE YOU TO
MYSELF; THAT WHERE I AM, THERE YOU MAY BE
ALSO."

"AND WHERE I GO YOU KNOW, AND THE WAY
YOU KNOW."

THOMAS SAID TO HIM, "LORD, WE DO NOT
KNOW WHERE YOU ARE GOING. HOW CAN WE
KNOW THE WAY?"

JESUS SAID TO HIM, "I AM THE WAY, THE
TRUTH, AND THE LIFE; NO ONE COMES TO THE
FATHER EXCEPT THROUGH ME.

JOHN 14:1-6

Your Truth, Your Life, Your Way

Father, Your blessings are easy to see:
The meadow, the blossoms, the birds in the tree.

Whether walking with others or walking alone,
I feel in my heart that You're setting the tone
To bless me, as You test me;

And, every day, I pray:
To see Your truth,
To live Your life,
And learn to walk Your way.

NAOMI TERRANELLA

Your Will

Help me, Lord, to bless someone
And be of use today.
Let Your light to others shine;
In Jesus' name, I pray.

Provide for me a mission
To spread Your Holy Word,
To share with those who'd listen
The wonders I have heard.

Guide me to find Your lost ones
And lead them to Your throne
To have the gifts You gave to me,
The finest ever known.

All of Your gracious wonders
Make worldly pleasures dirt.
Our sins You've cast asunder.
We're saved from endless hurt.

So, Lord, just let me be there
To answer when You call;
As You have been for me each time
I stumble, slip, and fall.

Let me be a comfort
To the lonely, sick, and lame,
To be a friend in time of need
And glorify Your name.

RONALD TERRANELLA

FINALLY, BRETHREN, WHATEVER THINGS
ARE TRUE, WHATEVER THINGS ARE NOBLE,
WHATEVER THINGS ARE JUST, WHATEVER
THINGS ARE PURE, WHATEVER THINGS ARE
LOVELY, WHATEVER THINGS ARE OF GOOD
REPORT, IF THERE IS ANY VIRTUE, AND THERE
IS ANYTHING PRAISEWORTHY, MEDITATE ON
THESE THINGS.

PHILIPPIANS 4:8

PEACE I LEAVE WITH YOU. MY PEACE I GIVE TO
YOU; NOT AS THE WORLD GIVES DO I GIVE TO
YOU. LET NOT YOUR HEART BE TROUBLED,
NEITHER LET IT BE AFRAID.

JOHN 14:27

www.ingramcontent.com/pod-product-compliance
Lightning Source LLC
Chambersburg PA
CBHW071355120626
46546CB00002B/695